Forty Win

A Potted Panto, very vaguely
"The Sleeping Beauty", by

RICHARD TYDEMAN

Samuel French - London
New York - Toronto - Hollywood

CHARACTERS

The Compere

The King

The Queen

Leading Fairy

Second Fairy

Third Fairy

Maud, *a Wicked Fairy*

A Soldier

Beauty, *a Princess*

A Nurse

Charley

A Prince

Scene: The King's Palace

(Production Note at end of play)

© 1956 by Richard Tydeman

Rights of Performance by Amateurs are controlled by Samuel French Ltd, 52 Fitzroy Street, London W1P 6JR, and they, or their authorized agents, issue licences to amateurs on payment of a fee. **It is an infringement of the Copyright to give any performance or public reading of the play before the fee has been paid and the licence issued.**

The Royalty Fee indicated below is subject to contract and subject to variation at the sole discretion of Samuel French Ltd.

Basic fee for each and every
perfomance by amateurs   Code B
in the British Isles

ISBN 0 573 06616 7

FORTY WINKS BEAUTY

The COMPERE *appears before the curtain carrying a full copy of the script, to which he refers from time to time.*

COMPERE. Kind friends, as your announcer, it is now my pleasant duty
> To introduce our Potted Panto, "Forty Winks for Beauty".
> Our scene's the palace of the King of nowhere in particular,
> (The floors are horizontal and the walls are perpendicular)
> But more important far than all these solid bricks and mortar,
> The King and Queen have organised a party for their daughter.

(Curtain up, revealing KING *and* QUEEN *standing by cot, and three or more* FAIRIES.*)*

> And round the small Princess's cot in dresses white and glistening,
> The Fairies have all gathered with their presents for the christening.

FAIRY 1. My present for the baby is a nature sweet and gentle,
And may she like all novels that are super-sentimental.

FAIRY 2. I wish the baby goodness that will never need correction.

FAIRY 3. And I wish she may ever have a *real* schoolgirl complexion.

KING. We thank you, Fairies, kindly for your gifts and your good wishes.

QUEEN. And please accept with compliments these silver-plated dishes.

(Enter MAUD, *a wicked Fairy, enveloped in a black cloak.)*

COMPERE. But who is this with face so fierce, and eyes as black as pitch?
It is the wicked fairy Maud, a nasty-tempered—witch.

MAUD. Ho, ho! And so you thought you wouldn't ask me to the party.

KING. We—thought that you were ill.

MAUD   Oh no, I'm very hale and hearty.

KING. Well, all the same, we're glad you came.

COMPERE (aside). Oh what a whopper!

KING (to QUEEN). Mabel,
Just run and tell the maids to lay another place at table.

MAUD. And now I'd like a silver dish just like you gave the others.

QUEEN. Oh dear, oh dear, there *was* one here—

KING. I took it round to Mother's.

COMPERE. But Maud is in a temper now, and with a smile unpleasant,
She turns towards the helpless babe and gives a fatal present:

MAUD. I wish your brat may prick her little finger on a spindle
And die of slow blood-poisoning. Goodbye. (*She starts to go.*)

KING. Here, that's a swindle!
We can't have that.

MAUD. Then put it in your pipe and have a smoke.
(*Goes out.*)

QUEEN. Oh, heavens above!

KING. Don't worry, love. It's just her little joke.

FAIRY 1. I sadly fear, your Majesty, it's not a joke, it's tragic.

KING. Well, can't you Fairies cancel out the spell with other magic?

COMPERE. The Fairies all look serious and go into a huddle,
To see if they can find a good solution to the muddle.
At last the leading Fairy speaks:

FAIRY 1. We cannot break the spell.

COMPERE. This Makes the King so mad.

KING. I wish old Maud would go to—

COMPERE. Well,
The Fairies in the corner have another little natter,
And then they say:

FAIRY 2. To break a spell is not an easy matter.
Make no mistake, we cannot break this spell, and nor can you.
But we can bend it quite a bit.

COMPERE. And that is what they do.

FAIRIES (*dancing in a ring*).
Eeny meeny, teeny weeny, shut the door and lock it.
Maskelyne and Robin Hood, John Bourne and Davy Crockett;

4

These are names to conjure with, as anyone can tell,
So here we call upon them all to help us bend the spell.

(*They stop and put their heads together whispering. The* KING *and* QUEEN *clasp each other in terror.*)

COMPERE. At last the Fairies straighten up, their magic task completed.
The leader speaks:

FAIRY 1. Your Majesty, old Maud is now defeated;
The Princess will not really die, in spite of all your fears,
But now instead she'll go to bed and sleep a hundred years.

QUEEN. A hundred years!

COMPERE. The Queen in tears upon the sofa sinks.
The King upon his fingers counts:

KING. That's forty *thousand* winks!

FAIRY 1. At your behest we've done our best, and there we'll have to stand.
So now, goodbye.

COMPERE. And off they fly, back home to Fairyland.

(*Exeunt* FAIRIES.)

(*The* KING *has been scribbling on a paper; he now claps his hands, and a* SOLDIER *enters.*)

The King now calls his Chief of Staff and gives him urgent orders.

KING. This proclamation go and make throughout our royal borders.

(SOLDIER *takes paper from* KING *and reads it.*)

SOLDIER. "Let every spindle, spinning wheel and sharply pointed thing,
Howe'er employed, be now destroyed. By Order. Signed, the King.
P.S. Whoever disobeys, or man, or maid, or wife,
Shall have his head cut off and then be sent to jail for life." (*Salutes and goes out.*)

COMPERE. So there we'll draw the curtain on the tragic royal pair;
And leave the little Princess crying:

BEAUTY (*off, in baby voice*). Nyair! Nyair! Nyair!

(*The Curtain falls, leaving* COMPERE *outside.*)

5

Act Two

COMPERE. The years have quickly rolled away, as years so often do;
So we'll exclude the interlude and pass on to Act Two.
The Princess has been growing fast, and I'm prepared to wager
In all your days you'll never gaze on such a cute teen-ager.

(*Curtain up. The cot has disappeared, and* BEAUTY *is sitting on sofa centre.*)

BEAUTY. My Dad's a very cruel man, he says I can't go walking
Without my Nurse. It's such a curse—but what's the use of talking?
I wish my Fairy Godmother would come and set me free.

COMPERE. The words are hardly spoken when, defying lock and key,
Through walls of brick twelve inches thick, and doors of stout oak board,
Appears someone we've met before:

(*Enter* MAUD, *with a spindle.*)

MAUD.   I am your Auntie Maud.

BEAUTY. You've come to set me free?

MAUD.   No no.

COMPERE.   Her hopes begin to dwindle.

MAUD. I've brought a present for you.

BEAUTY.   Oh, what is it?

MAUD.   A spindle.

COMPERE. Alas, the fatal implement the Princess takes in hand.
She does not fear the danger here; she does not understand.

MAUD. Go on dear, feel how sharp it is.

COMPERE.   Ah Princess, have a care!

MAUD. Place one small joint upon the point, and press it.

BEAUTY (*pricking herself*).   Oh!

MAUD.   There, there.

BEAUTY. I feel so faint.

MAUD.   Of course you do. Lie down upon this bed.

(BEAUTY *lies on sofa.*)

Revenge at last! She's going fast. She'll very soon be dead.

COMPERE. The wicked fairy dances round with fiendish laughs and jeers,

6

Then quits the room and mounts her broom, and simply
   disappears. *(Goes out.)*
And now the young Princess's Nurse, attracted by the din,
All out of breath and scared to death, comes quickly
   bursting in.
                  (Enter NURSE.*)*

NURSE. Princess, Princess!

COMPERE.   In great distress, like some demented thing.

NURSE. My child, my child!

COMPERE.   In accents wild, she makes the welkin ring.

NURSE. Oh, art thou feeling faint my dear, or is it indigestion?
   Or art thou dead upon thy bed?

COMPERE *(aside).*   And that's the Guinea Question!
            *(*NURSE *beckons. Enter* SOLDIER.*)*
The Nurse then calls the Chief of Staff, who calls the
   King again,

*(*SOLDIER *beckons. Enter* KING, *who beckons.)*

Who calls his spouse. *(Enter* QUEEN.*)* They try to rouse
   their daughter, but in vain.
Then suddenly the Queen espies the spindle on the floor.

QUEEN. Who dares to bring this deadly thing within the palace
   door?

COMPERE. The others all examine it like Customs-house officials;

KING. What's this I see? M.A.U.D.—the Fairy Maud's initials?

COMPERE. So now the horrid truth is out, confirming all their fears:
   The Princess gay is doomed to stay asleep a hundred
   years.

QUEEN. If only we could sleep as well!

COMPERE.   The Queen in anguish cries.
                  (Enter FAIRY 1.*)*

FAIRY 1. No sooner said than done!

COMPERE.   And in the leading Fairy flies.

FAIRY 1. Now sit down please. Be quite at ease. You'll soon be
   fast asleep.
   And round the wall a forest tall shall constant vigil keep.
            (She looks down at BEAUTY.*)*
   So slumber on, fair Beauty, till to wake you with a kiss
   A Prince shall come.

SOLDIER *(holding up spindle).* Excuse me, Mum, what shall I do
   with this?

COMPERE. And though the Fairy could have made an answer, that's
   quite certain,

7

> Her breath she saves, her wand she waves, and down
> comes sleep—and curtain.

(They are all asleep, and FAIRY 1 *trips off, as the curtain falls leaving* COMPERE *outside as before.)*

ACT THREE

COMPERE. Now Father Time accelerates to super-sonic pace;
> And past our ears a hundred years have flown without a
> trace.
> Around the palace, holly trees and prickly brambles sway;
> No mortals dare to venture there—" 'tis haunted," so
> they say.
> And there, alas, our story ends, for up until tonight,
> Through all these years, no Prince appears, to put our
> troubles right.
> And whether in the future any Prince will come or no,
> I cannot tell. And so, farewell, and thank you.

CHARLEY *(from back of audience).*   'arf a mo!

> (CHARLEY *advances to the front, and mounts the stage. He
> is dressed in "Teddy-boy" style, with cigarette drooping from
> corner of mouth.)*

COMPERE. But who is this who looks as if he needs a dose of physic,
> With coat so long, and accent strong?

CHARLEY.   I'm Charley Prince of Chiswick.

COMPERE. Thrice welcome Prince, and have you come to break the
> ancient curse
> Imposed by Maud, and snap the cord of sleep that
> binds us?

CHARLEY.   Yers.

COMPERE. But can you take a sword in hand, and can you cut a dash,
> And wake the Sleeping Beauty?

CHARLEY.   I dunno, I'll 'ave a bash.

COMPERE. But how to hack through jungle black—that really is a
> poser—
> And reach the gate?

CHARLEY.   That's easy, mate, I drive me own bull-dozer.

COMPERE *(aside).*
> This Charley is not quite the sort of Prince they have in
> books;
> But possibly he may not be as dopey as he looks.

(To CHARLEY.)
> Away, then, noble Charley Prince, and break
> spell.

8

(CHARLEY *goes out into wings.*)

So off he goes. And I suppose we'd better go as well,
And see just what's been happening within the portico
Where last we saw those sleepers, just a hundred years
ago.

(*Curtain up, disclosing the sleepers, still in the same positions, but cobwebs now hang round and above them.*)

How cruel Time has laid his hand upon this little scene!
On all asleep the dust lies deep. I'll show you what I
mean:

(COMPERE *blows top of* SOLDIER'S *head and a cloud of dust rises from it.*)

The spider has been busy, too, and spinning finest laces,
Has left the ground and hung them round in most
peculiar places.

(COMPERE *removes a cobweb from the* KING'S *face, etc.*)

But now the noble Charley Prince, bull-dozing through
the trees,

(*Re-enter* CHARLEY.)

Arrives within the Palace walls, and gasps at what he sees.
Say now, Your Royal Highness, sir—or "Charley" if
you'd rather,
What do you think?

CHARLEY (*looking at* KING). Cor strike me pink, the ghost of
'amlet's father!

COMPERE. Come, please approach as tenderly and softly as you may,
And gently plant a loving kiss on Beauty's lips.

CHARLEY (*moving up behind* BEAUTY'S *couch*).   O.K.

COMPERE. Now are you ready, noble Prince?

CHARLEY.   I've got me lips all pursed.

COMPERE. If you don't mind, it might be kind to take your fag out
first.

(CHARLEY *removes cigarette.*)

In silence let us gaze upon this scene of purest bliss,
As Charley P., on bended knee, wakes Beauty with a kiss.

(CHARLEY *kisses* BEAUTY. *All wake and stretch.* BEAUTY *does not see* CHARLEY *who is behind her as she sits up*).

KING (*yawning*). Ah, what's the time?

SOLDIER.   Your Majesty, my watch has stopped at five.

KING.   It feels so late. Oh, what a state!

9

QUEEN.   Come husband, look alive;
It's Friday, I must get some fish, and you must pay the wages.

KING.   I feel so stiff, it's just as if I'd been asleep for ages.

BEAUTY.   Oh where—?—

NURSE.   Don't interrupt, my dear, just beg your Daddy's pardon.
And now you know, it's time to go for walkies in the garden;
So upsy-daisy.

BEAUTY (*looking round*). Go away. Where is he? Where's my Prince?
That best of men who kissed me then?

CHARLEY.   I've been 'ere ever since.

BEAUTY.   I mean the Prince who rescued me.

CHARLEY.   That's right.

BEAUTY.   It wasn't *you?*

CHARLEY.   It *was,* you know.

BEAUTY.   Oh say not so! It simply can't be true.

COMPERE.   Princess, the young man speaks the truth. It happened as he said.
Now will you take him for your mate, and will you with him wed?

BEAUTY.   That little pest? If that's the best this century can show,
Then pass me up the spindle, I'll go back to sleep.

(*Enter a real* PRINCE, *dressed in traditional princely style.*)

PRINCE.   No, no!

COMPERE.   Now just a minute, first of all, before we all get dizzy,
Please tell us who you are.

PRINCE.   I am a Royal Prince.

CHARLEY.   Oh, *is* he?

PRINCE.   Your Highness, I am here at last. I'm sorry I was late
Some silly pig had parked a big bull-dozer in the gate.
I got my men to push it in the castle moat, and so
My coach and four are at the door. Come Princess, shall we go?

BEAUTY.   Most gladly.

CHARLEY.   I say, wait a bit!

COMPERE.   But Charley pleads in vain.
The King and Queen their blessing give, and tripping in again,

10

(*Enter the* FAIRIES, *including* MAUD.)

The Fairies all, both short and tall, bring presents for
the Bride;
Except old Maud, who's quite ignored.

MAUD.   Once more I am defied!
On one condition only, the Princess can go free—
And that is if the Prince who kissed her lips shall marry
me!
(*She opens her arms towards the* PRINCE.)

PRINCE.   Agreed.
BEAUTY.   Agreed. } (*They push* CHARLEY *into* MAUD'S *arms.*)

CHARLEY.   'ere, wait a bit!

COMPERE.   But there's no time to parley;
So Beauty gets a proper Prince, and Maud a proper
Charley.

(*The Curtains close, then immediately open again, and the
players come forward in couples to make their bows to the
audience and then go into the wings or walk down through the
hall. The* PRINCE *and* BEAUTY *come first, and then the* KING *and*
QUEEN, *and the* SOLDIER *and* NURSE. *The* FAIRIES *follow in
pairs, the last pair—or odd one—holds out a hand to the*
COMPERE *who accompanies them, with a wink at the audience.*
CHARLEY *and* MAUD *are left alone. Suddenly* MAUD *throws off
her enveloping black cloak, revealing sweater and slacks, or
similar clothes of gaudy pattern, flashy jewellery, etc., so that she
looks exactly the female counterpart to* CHARLEY. *They embrace
and march off together, arm in arm.*

THE END

11

PRODUCTION NOTE

This is intended to be a complete "rag" and should be played as such —and the "hammier" the better. No attempt should be made at realism, but of course it is important for the players to speak the exact lines allotted to them, no more and no less; otherwise the impact of the atrocious verse will be lost.

Setting can be as simple or elaborate as you like. The only essential pieces of furniture are a sofa or couch (or three chairs in a row!) for BEAUTY to lie on, and a cot. (Act One only.)

Costumes can easily be concocted from wardrobe, dressing-up box and rag-bag. The royal family should have cardboard crowns, and the SOLDIER something that looks like uniform. CHARLEY and MAUD are described in the text.

Silver dishes can be tin plates or cardboard plates painted silver. An old chair leg makes an admirable spindle. Cobwebs can be made out of thick string, or wire, or even painted on pieces of paper and pinned to the walls. The effect of blowing dust from the SOLDIER's head can be obtained by depositing a small heap of powder on his head before the curtain rises on Act Three.

The COMPERE can best be described as a cross between a Circus Ring-master and a B.B.C. Announcer—with a dash of the Music Hall Chairman thrown in.

Don't worry if you have not enough men or women to make a balanced cast, nobody will mind. Good luck to all who try it!

RICHARD TYDEMAN.